God at Work

by

John Goldingay

Principal, St John's College, Nottingham

and

Robert Innes

Theological Researcher and
Part-time Tutor at St John's College, Durham

GROVE BOOKS LIMITED
Bramcote Nottingham NG9 3DS

Contents

Editorial Preface 2

1. God at Work in Genesis 1 3

    God the First Worker 3

    God's Creativity: Artist, Whirlwind, Spoken Word 4

    God's Work: the Whole, the Parts, the Goal 5

    Image and Gospel, Power and Love 6

    Power and Empowerment 9

    Work, Rest and Play 10

2. The Modern Problem of Work 12

3. The Demographics of Work 13

4. Called to Work: Luther's Doctrine of Vocation 14

5. Ideas about Work in the Modern Period 16

6. Towards a Contemporary Theology of Work 20

The Cover Illustration is by Greg Forster after William Blake

Editorial Preface

The idea of publishing a number of Grove Booklets on the subject of 'Work' is largely the outcome of the 1993 Anglican Evangelical Assembly (AEA), which took 'Work' as its main theme. The first part of this booklet contains the Bible exposition on 'God at Work in Genesis 1' given at the conference by John Goldingay, Principal and Old Testament lecturer at St John's College, Nottingham. The second part contains my own reflections as a systematic theologian and former businessman. We intend to publish a second booklet in the Grove Ethics series which will present the thoughts of the Rt Revd David Sheppard, a bishop well known for his concern for urban and industrial affairs, and (writing in a personal capacity) James Allcock, Director of Gas Supplies at British Gas. The approach of this present booklet is deliberately theological; the follow-up booklet will contain more practical reflections from the coalface (or the pipeline) of British industrial life. Ways in which churches can pastorally and spiritually support working people have been developed in a third booklet, produced in the Grove Pastoral Series in March 1994, by Rt Revd Graham Dow, another of the main speakers at AEA. We hope that the three booklets between them will provide a lively and wide-ranging contribution to a subject that has until recently been largely neglected in church circles.

Robert Innes

First Impression July 1994
ISSN 0951-2667
ISBN 1 85174 272 7

1
God at Work in Genesis 1

It is marvellous for our theme that at the very beginning of the Bible is God doing a week's work. Further, it is a week which comes to one of its climaxes when God puts human beings into the world to reflect God's own being there, to represent God; and the image of God in which human beings are made is the image of a worker.

In our culture work is characteristically something we do for money. Work is defined as employment. When we come to scripture we expect it to broaden our understanding of things, and with regard to work it does so immediately. The very first chapter of scripture is about work, and it subverts our understanding of the matter. Work is not essentially a commodity which ordinary people sell to human bosses. That way of looking at work is a means of people being oppressed, whether they are people who have some of this commodity which they can sell or whether they are not. Work is not employment. If we can see something of what work means for God, even though God is self-employed as vicars used to be, we may be able to see something of what it might mean for us. We may also be helped as we seek to formulate a vision regarding work in what is for many people a post-employment world.

God the First Worker

'In the beginning God created the heavens and the earth.' There are already some hints of the significance of this week's work in those opening words. When do we think God started working? Was it when Joshua was given the land, or when Moses and his people were given their freedom, or when Abraham and Sarah were given hope for the future? Scripture can see all of those as the beginning of God's work. But Genesis invites us to a much more fundamental view of the work of God. It goes back to the beginning. Labour and paid work were invented after the fall, but human beings had real work to do in the Garden of Eden, because they were made in the image of God the worker.

God's work goes back to the beginning, and it is a programme which is quite all-encompassing. It embraces the heavens and the earth, embraces everything in its entirety. Before we are told any of the detail of God's work, each of its individual aspects is already set in the context of a whole. What God does each day could otherwise be seen as a discrete whole, and indeed it is that, but it is also part of something greater to which each individual part eventually contributes. It is important for our understanding of our individual work to see it as part of some whole. No-one wants to be a mere cog in a machine whose total nature they cannot appreciate or envisage.

There are hints here and elsewhere in scripture that God operates according to the rules of management by objectives. At the beginning God stands back from the project of creating a totality called the heavens and the earth, puts a day off into the heavenly diary, then divides what needs to be done into six bite-sized chunks, allocates one to each day, and works through them systematically.

Or perhaps God is more charismatic than that. Many leaders like flying by the seat of their pants, playing things off the cuff, trusting hunches, and much of the scriptural story indicates that God also does that, trying something out and working out afterwards how it fits into a pattern. Sometimes God works like an old-fashioned band which went into the studio with all its songs rehearsed so that it could record them straight over two days, but sometimes God works like the opulent rock-star who spends months in the studio jamming and discovering what comes out. God tries creating light and sky, land and sea, then stands back from them and says, 'O, that's nice, I'll keep that'. God creates, works, with a combination of purpose and playfulness, spontaneity and system.

God's Creativity: Artist, Whirlwind, Spoken Word

God 'creates'. Much is made of that word, and rightly. It appears in scripture only with God as subject. Admittedly that may be a misleading fact; if Israelites wanted to speak of human creativity, I imagine 'create' would be the word they used, as is the case today. After all, when we talk about God, we usually do so by using language for human activity and stretching it to apply to God. We can do so because of the very fact that we as human beings are made in God's image, which means that language which applies to the image can be used for the original. Presumably that applies to the language of creativity. Human beings create, and it is one of the most extraordinary things they do, so the language is also naturally used of God, in the conviction that our creativity reflects God's.

Creativity suggests the mysterious, joyful, magical, moment when a person brings something into being out of nothing—a painting or a pot, a bridge or a car. There were raw materials from which these things were made, but they seem quite insignificant in the light of the gulf between them and what someone has created from them.

God's work, too, was creative. At first there was nothing, or a formless, shapeless, dark waste. Then God set to work, and there was a created wonder.

What makes the difference? Part of the answer is that the spirit of God was hovering over the face of the waters. That is an enigmatic observation. The spirit of God is the tumultuous, gusting, divine whirlwind which lifts Elijah or Ezekiel and wafts them from one place to another, the supernatural invisible but irresistible gale of God which whips up seas and flattens trees without us being able to see whence it comes or whither it goes, but which can be the agent of new creativity. Elijah, Ezekiel, John the Baptist, Jesus—something inexplicable, tumultuous, unpredictable, creative is here.

In the light of that, it is enigmatic to talk about the spirit-wind of God 'hovering'; tumultuous winds put the hovercraft out of service. The word 'hover' is used only once more in scripture, of the vulture hovering over its young in Deuteronomy 32, and perhaps that is significant. There again is a being of soar-

4

ing and dangerous power, but one capable of exercising its power for positive, even gentle ends. When God does a week's work, tumultuous resources are harnessed to divine creativity, as with the harnessing of nuclear power.

So far God's work has been described by means of two powerful images, the creativity of the artist and the energy of the whirlwind. Now there is a third image, the spoken word. God's first act was to speak. 'Can't we have some light around here?' said God: and there was light. Why?

There is a certain inevitability about it. As long as God was one step away from this inchoate world there could be darkness here, but once God started becoming personally concerned with it, looking at it, and talking about it, darkness was bound to be replaced by light. Once God is there, there cannot but be light. But God also consciously wills it. 'Let's have some light here,' says God. And there is, by the mysterious, magical power of words.

Words are indeed mysteriously, magically powerful. That is not true of all words. Not everyone's words are powerful. But when the person is powerful for one reason or another, the words are. So when someone you love says 'I love you', or someone you have wronged says 'That's OK', or a minister says 'I baptize you', or the admissions tutor says 'Yes, you can come to this college', or Jesus says 'Your sins are forgiven' or 'Little girl, get up', their words are dynamically effective. They have power to do things. They are like magic. We talk about magic when something happens and we cannot see how it could have been made to happen, we cannot see the links; the magician does something, there is a puff of smoke, and something amazing has taken place. So it is when God is at work. God says something and light replaces darkness, healing replaces sickness, forgiveness replaces guilt. All God does is speak. Speech is of the essence of work; it is how God works. It is another way to describe God working magic, alongside the ideas of God's being creative and of God's spirit being let loose in the world. The question then is how we encourage work to involve speech, how we encourage workers to work by speaking.

God's Work: the Whole, the Parts and the Goal

God, then, sets about a week's work, bringing into being light and sky, land and seas, vegetation and fruit, sun and moon and stars. The way God went about this work was both holistic and analytic. The way the story is told, I have suggested, there was a whole in mind from the beginning. The parts are on the way to being a whole. At the same time, the parts are brought into being one by one as God keeps separating one thing from another. There is an intuitive, holistic aspect to God's work, and an analytic, rational aspect. These two aspects of work go together; they are complementary, not rivals.

What more shall I say? Time fails me to tell of the swarms of living creatures and the birds flying across the firmament of heaven and the animals of the wild and the cattle and the creeping things, the beings who came into existence because God thought things out, had moments of inspiration, set to work, exercised creativity, and brought something good into being. Though perhaps we should reflect on the significance of the fact that the concern of God's work was the bringing into being of a world of living beings, a world characterized by order and beauty, by diversity and ecology.

Perhaps that provides us with criteria for evaluating our own work. It is easy to make cheap points about the way development and industrialization have spoilt the creation and imperilled the planet, but at least we may note the general point that the result—and the implicit goal—of God's week of work was to bring into being a created world characterized by beauty, order, diversity, and mutuality. It had to be that way because the work reflected the nature of the worker, for God is characterized—among other things—by beauty, order, diversity, and mutuality. Those features of God's aims and achievements suggest criteria for our evaluation of our own work as financiers or homemakers, ministers or manufacturers, theologians, smallholders, or whatever: to bring into being a world characterized by beauty, order, diversity, and mutuality.

Yet all those creatures, though well-attested by their place of intrinsic significance in God's purpose, were not the climax of God's project, since God had foreseen something better for us, that apart from us they should not be made perfect. The magician saves the most mind-blowing trick, the *pièce de resistance*, for the climax of the programme. Having brought into being all the manifold species of the animal world, God says 'Now let's create a being on earth who is the mirror image of us in heaven'.

'Let us create'. It is a nice question who the 'us' is. We now know that the God who was making the world was Father, Son, and Holy Spirit, and Luther therefore assumed that here the members of the Trinity are talking to each other, but Calvin recognizes that in Genesis this is anachronistic. God knew about being the Trinity, but Genesis and its original audience did not. What did the God who inspired scripture expect that audience to learn from this 'us'?

What is most significant is simply the fact that this moment when human beings are about to be created is marked as a moment of special reflection. God stands back from work half way through the day, in the way executives do if they are to think creatively and have new ideas, not be bound by the parameters of what they have been doing already and be sucked into mere maintenance rather than creativity. Up go God's feet onto the desk for ten minutes after lunch, and there on Friday afternoon when anyone else is preoccupied with getting away a bit early for the weekend, emerges this amazing idea. 'How about including among the population of this planet some people who are actually just like God, and letting them be in control of all the other creatures?'

Image and Gospel, Power and Love

Why did God do this? Indeed, why did God create the world at all? The story gives no direct answer, but may contain some implicit ones. A hundred years ago a Babylonian creation story was discovered and it was declared that the Genesis story had been taken from it. It was a strange theory because the two are so different. What can more plausibly be seen sometimes is the Genesis story confronting what the Babylonians believed, or even making fun of it.

Some of the events in Genesis 1 come in a surprising order. Sun, moon, and stars are created only on Day Four. Israel knew as well as we do that the sequence of darkness and light on Day One presupposes the existence and the movement of sun, moon, and stars. So how can Genesis speak of darkness and light before it speaks of sun, moon, and stars? Now the Israelites also knew that the Babylonians believed that sun, moon, and stars actually decided the destiny of the world. They took them too seriously. So in God's week's work sun, moon, and stars are demoted; they do not even appear until over half way through, to show how insignificant they actually are. Light and time are the gifts of God. God may choose to put lamp-posts in the sky to be the means of our receiving light and time, but they are significantly subordinate entities. They are not to be taken too seriously. They are not even named, except as lamp-posts. What the Genesis story learned from the Babylonian one was some of its strange ideas which needed confronting, and which the people of God needed to be wary of.

What the Babylonian story says about the reasons for creating human beings also illustrates the point. There had been a major fight among the gods and they are rather tired. One of them then has the bright idea of creating creatures called 'human beings' who 'will be charged with the service of the gods that they might be at ease'. So they make a 'plan for the relief of the gods', which involves recycling some bits of the god who led the losing side in the battle: and 'out of his blood they fashioned humanity'. The chief of the gods 'imposed the service and let free the gods', says the story.[1]

There is thus an irony in saying that human beings were created as God's mirror image. The Babylonians also believed that. They knew from their own experience how human life was characterized by violence, frustration, and disenchantment, by rivalry and conflict between the sexes, and when they told stories about the life of heaven, they assumed it was the same. The gods were involved in violence, frustration, disenchantment, rivalry, and sexual conflict. When they created human beings, they created them out of bits of one of the more violent of these gods. That is where we as human beings came from, on the Babylonian theory. It is not at all surprising that our human life is characterized by instincts such as violence and sexual conflict. It reflects the raw material we were made from. We are created in the divine image. We are a mirror image of that kind of god. Chaos on earth reflects chaos in heaven. It is built into the structure of reality. That is what Babylonian religion told its people.

Alongside that Genesis 1 offers a gospel, one that agrees that we were created as a mirror image of God, but declares that God is a very different being from what the Babylonians thought. The Babylonian gods have absolute power over the world, but at the same time they are powerless because they are at such odds with each other. The real God, the God whom Israel knows, is one who is in actual control, because there are no rivals to this God's power. The one who in

1   *Ancient Near Eastern Texts*, ed J B Pritchard, p 68.

cool and orderly fashion took a week over bringing into being this whole universe and any other universes that exist, this God has real power, real authority, real control of the situation.

Potentially that is frightening. Absolute power is frightening. That could include absolute power exercised by God. But this is a different kind of God.

Power is a little like wealth. You do not have to feel guilty about finding yourself in possession of it, as long as you use it to give it away, use it for other people's benefit. It is a commonplace today to say that there is nothing wrong with power as long as we use it to empower other people. We can see that as a feature of the way God goes about work. What God does is use power to empower other workers. God gives power away to them.

Something like that was a feature built into God's creation project from Day One. When things started (Jürgen Moltmann points out in his book *God in Creation*), or rather before things started, God was all there was, God was everything. When God set about creating the world, the first thing God had to do was accept a degree of self-limitation. God had to withdraw from being everything in order to make room for something else to be. The self-emptying that came to a climax with the cross did not begin with the incarnation but with creation, with the creation of anything.

To put it another way, creation was an act of love. That week's work on God's part was an expression of the love of God sharing the life of God with a new world. Creation is not just an expression of power but an expression of love. 'In created things lies the forgiveness of sins', Luther said. In other words, in creation you see the footprints of the God whom you know as the God of grace, mercy and forgiveness. God's week's work was an act of costly love.

This self-emptying is extended when God creates human beings with a degree of independence, more like grown-up children than little children, and shares power in the world with them. God does not merely use the workforce. God empowers it. 'How about making human beings as mirror images of God, and letting them have authority over the fish and the birds, the cattle and the reptiles—over all the world really, might as well go the whole hog,' says God.

It was wonderfully risky and irresponsible. When people give power to the workers, they take a chance on everything going horribly wrong. Indeed, God has the resources to run a computer projection and discover that it is odds on that it will indeed go horribly wrong. One of the theories about who is being addressed when God says 'Let us make humanity in our image' is that God is consulting the angels. It is possible to imagine the angels' response. 'Give these human beings authority and power in this world that you have not even finished creating yet? Are you off your chariot? Look at what happened with that Lucifer character. And you are thinking of giving power to that lot?' God does it anyway. That is how committed God is to worker participation. The process is as important to God as the end product. The people and their involvement is as important as what gets produced. God will sacrifice production levels for the sake of collaborative working.

So the idea that human beings were created to serve God is present in Genesis as it is in the Babylonian story, but the atmosphere is quite different. When human beings are created to rule the world on God's behalf, God is not just using them. God gives power to them.

Power and Empowerment

God recognizes that this future workforce is a collection of people who are of similar nature to their boss. God does not look down from the office across the factory floor and see the workforce as like a collection of units, things, aliens, or enemies. God sees them as people of the same nature. They are not merely things that God has created. They are people.

The 'they' are both men and women, and the world of work for which they are created embraces both what we think of as the world of work, out there, and the world of the home, the domestic world. Here is another point at which Genesis subverts our sinful understanding of work as equivalent to being employed by someone for monetary payment. It is men and women together who are created as God's mirror image to share jointly in God's work project, in the world of the home and the world out there. It is only when we have men and women together that we have God's own nature reflected, in the work that goes on in the wide world, the work in the home, the work in the community, and the work in the church. It is men and women together, standing and working side by side, who have authority and power in God's world.

God's interest in process as well as production may again be significant here. In our culture, at least, women tend to be better at process, and arguably therefore one reason why the world of work is in a mess is that it is so shaped by men's values. One of the ways the fall deeply affects the world of work is by taking women out of it, redefining the world of work so that it is mostly a world that works in men's ways even when it does leave space for women to take part. It needs men and women working together at this point as at every other if God's image is to be reflected and mirrored in the world of work.

We reflect God's image in the way we control the world on God's behalf. Genesis says human beings are given power and authority over the world.

This should arouse suspicion. Genesis, after all, was written by human beings. The Babylonian story closes with God establishing kingship in the world; that is hardly surprising, for the Babylonian story was sponsored by the palace. It is a warrant for the power and authority of the king. The king can do what he likes because God put him there. Israel itself had no kings at the time this story was written. At its best Israel did not believe in having kings, just as the New Testament did not believe in bishops and vicars and so on. It believes everybody is created in God's image. It does not believe in a king reflecting the power of the divine king or a bishop or priest representing Jesus. So Israel's story ends up with God giving power and authority in the world to humanity as a whole.

But as I have hinted, this is hardly surprising. If camels had written the story, it would presumably have ended up with camels made in God's image. Is this another example of religion being used to buttress people in power? The Babylonian king used his story ideologically to justify his power; we use this story ideologically to justify our power. We can do what we deem fit to the world because God gave us authority in it, because we are made in his image.

There lies the snag, and the way the story subverts our ideological use of it. We are made in the divine image, made to reflect God's way of working in the world. God, we have seen, exercises power and authority, but exercises it in such a way as to give people and things space, give people and things their own authority. God uses power to empower. Genesis's picture of God at work subverts our ideological use of it to do what we like with the world in our work. The criterion it challenges us to apply is, in our work at home and in business, in manufacturing, in the church, and in the city, are we mirroring the God whose work was designed to give space, authority and power to the world?

Work, Rest and Play

There is one more point to be made. God's week comes to one climax on Friday with the creation of humanity. It then comes to a second climax on Saturday, when God's work has come to an end. The chapter divisions in the Bible obscure this fact that God's diary in Genesis 1 comes to an end not on Friday but on Saturday. 'On the seventh day God finished his work which he had done' and had a rest. 'So God blessed the sabbath day and hallowed it, because on the seventh day God rested from all his work which he had done in creation'.

It is a picture, and we cannot press it. When people complain that Jesus is working on Saturday, because he heals somebody, he snorts 'My father is still at work even though it is Saturday, so don't complain if I am' (John 5.17). On the first Saturday the sun still shone, the rain still fell, and the vegetables still grew. They do not do this automatically, but because God makes them. God continues working on Saturday, doing what has to be done. It cannot all be left till Sunday. God is not a legalist.

There is, however, an important point in the picture of God stopping working, indeed more than one. In its context, there was originally another fragment of gospel here for Israelites troubled by Babylonians. The Babylonians did not treat Saturday as a holy day, and perhaps laughed at Jews for doing so. That would have made Jews start asking questions about themselves and their own faith. Why do we stop everything on Friday night and light the sabbath candles and try to make the next 24 hours different? Is it just a peculiarity of our religion—the Babylonians have theirs, the Canaanites have theirs, and we have ours? Israelites lived all their lives in a multi-faith context, like us, and faced the same questions.

Genesis 1 gives them an answer. No, keeping Saturday special is not merely your peculiarity, any more than the kosher laws and circumcision. They really were God's gifts to you, signs of God's love. They were designed to show something forth to the world. There was a pattern in the way God set about the work of creating the world. It had a beginning, a middle, and an end. Each day God sat back in the evening, looked over what had been achieved, and said, 'Well, that's not bad, is it? I rather like that'; and there was a moment when the basic creative work had been completed and God sat back for a whole day and made Saturday special. So that is why you yourselves keep Saturday special, the story said to Israel in exile. It is not merely your religious peculiarity. It reflects something about God's pattern of work.

It is not that God is tired at the end of the week; that is not the reason for the Sabbath. God did not find that first week's work was horrendously taxing. It was not laborious. You do not rest because you are tired. You rest because you have completed a job and it is time to sit back and enjoy it. Sometimes when we go on holiday it takes a week to unwind and we start actually enjoying relaxation only in the second week. That is a sign that work has become a tyranny. 'God does not spend the seventh day in exhaustion but in serenity and peace', Walter Brueggemann comments. For Israel the celebration of a day of rest was 'the announcement of trust in this God who is confident enough to rest. It was then and is now an assertion that life does not depend upon our feverish activity of self-securing, but that there can be a pause in which life is given to us simply as a gift'.

The sabbath confronted the culture. It still does. The gentile world, including the gentile Christian world, often seems to know very little about a pattern of work and repose of the kind that Genesis pictures and Judaism traditionally enjoys. It knows very little of a rhythm of activity and reflection, of creativity and sitting back looking over what you have done, enjoying it, admiring it, letting it be there, and being there yourself. We all need our ways of unwinding and refusing to be in bondage to the world of work, of safeguarding the presence of a rhythm of work and repose in our lives, a rhythm of activity and reflection, of creativity and sitting back. It is important because it is part of being human, and it is part of being human because it is part of being divine. It is part of being made in God's image, because God did not work a seven day week. God worked Sunday to Friday and then had Saturday off. The pattern of God's story says something to us as workers, and says something to us as people who influence patterns of work for other people.

God was the first worker. God's work was a whole. God worked both purposefully and playfully. God worked creatively. God worked with the unpredictable energy of the whirlwind. God worked magically, just by speaking. God worked, for beauty, order, beauty, and mutuality. God worked in order to give space to other people and to give power to them. God worked out of costly love and with costly love. God worked in way that cared for both process and production. God worked in a way that involved both women and men. God worked, but God also sat back and rested.

'In the beginning God created the heavens and the earth. And on the seventh day God finished his work'. But the Father of Jesus is still at work, and so is Jesus himself.

2
The Modern Problem of Work

It seems to me that one of the significant aspects of our country's present spiritual malaise is a crisis in our attitude to work. There are those, for example some post 'Big-Bang' workers in the City of London, who are so thrown into their work that they feel absorbed in it and perhaps by it. For others, work is experienced only as a source of disappointment, anxiety or stress. Graduates one or two years into their professions commonly express disillusionment with working life. Increasing numbers of middle ranking and senior executives are seeking early retirement. Social security and pension schemes (both good things in themselves) have partially weakened the *natural* link between work and survival. The ecological movement has seemingly undermined the *ethical* legitimacy of much of our industrial wealth creation.

Yet, despite our ambiguities, work remains of absolutely central importance to human life. Unemployment is experienced as a crushing blow to one's membership of society and indeed to one's very humanity. 'Work' is what most people spend most of their waking lives doing. What people actually *do* is more important for understanding them than what they say, or how they spend their money, or how they vote. Our *calling*, be it to parenthood, to accountancy or to the mission field, isn't just accidental; it is crucial to our identity.

The aim of this paper, therefore, is to offer some theological suggestions to help us understand our work and the modern secular workplace within the wider purposes of God. I begin (chapter 3) by setting out some basic statistics concerning the nature of work in our society. I then summarise Martin Luther's doctrine of vocation (chapter 4), a formulation that has been extremely influential and from which we can still profit greatly today. By contrast with Luther, I consider the attitudes to work characteristic of the Enlightenment and modern times (chapter 5).

This forms the background to a contemporary theology of work (chapter 6). I suggest that theology must start by affirming rather than withdrawing from the workplace. Such affirmation can only be sustained if we begin with a right understanding of God the Holy Trinity at work in his creation. I argue that, in the context of modern working life, this creative power is to be discerned especially in those 'corporate cultures' that promote creativity, contentment and justice.

3

The Demographics of Work

Some 68% of UK people in employment now work in 'services' compared with 30% in manufacturing and just 2% in agriculture.[1] Agricultural employment has been falling steadily for the last 150 years. The fall in numbers employed in manufacturing has, on the other hand, been sharpest in the last 20 years, with only 6 million employed in this sector in 1991 compared with nearly 10 million in 1971. Over this same 20 year period the numbers employed in services rose from around 11 million to around 15 million.

These figures do not represent a simple switch of employees from manufacturing to services. The fall in manufacturing employment reflects (typically male) job losses resulting from the serious slump in UK industry, whilst the increase in service sector employment is partly accounted for by the increasing female labour-participation rate. Certainly it is too simple to suggest that we are moving into a 'post-industrial society'.[2] Many of the 'services', such as transport, accountancy and retailing, are directly related to manufacturing. The economy of the UK as a whole remains crucially dependent on our manufacturing base.

Nonetheless, these changing employment patterns do indicate that relatively few employees are now involved in the basic, creative processes of growing and making things. Only a very few of us depend directly on the land for our living. An increasing proportion of those fortunate enough to have jobs are working in the worlds of financial services, tourism, education and health-care. We have been moving towards a more complex society in which a more sophisticated range of needs are being catered for.

This is of great significance for the church and for theology. It is no longer adequate only to discern the work of the Creator in the world of nature and agriculture. The embarrassment of the typical urban or suburban church about what its annual harvest festival means reflects this. We must also understand God's creativity to be disclosed in the richness and complexity of the wide range and sophistication of human working life.

A second set of demographic statistics emphasises this point about complexity. Despite all that is said about the importance of small enterprises, we actually live in a world dominated by the large corporations. Less than 20% of employees in the manufacturing sector, for example, work for small businesses. Across a range of key UK manufacturing areas the biggest 5 firms account for more than half of gross output.[3] At an international level the annual sales figures of the top

---

1   OECD Economic Survey for the UK 1990/91.
2   A term popularised by Daniel Bell in the late 60s and early 70s.
3   For example, the biggest 5 in their sector account for 61% of mineral oil processing, 95% of iron and steel production, 88% of motor vehicle building and 77% of aerospace equipment (*Business Monitor* 1990).

13

5 corporations are larger than the Gross Domestic Products of all but the largest western trading nations.[1] Our understanding of work must reckon with the sheer size, scale and power of the modern corporations. How are we to understand God to be at work precisely *here*?

4

Called to Work: Luther's Doctrine of Vocation

Luther was deeply influenced by 1 Cor 7.20 'Each in the calling in which he was called, in this let him remain'. These callings or states Luther called 'stations'. He took it that the natural occupations in which men or women find themselves when they become Christians are *good* and not to be renounced. His object, of course, was to attack the so-called 'double standard' whereby people might be persuaded to give up their current livelihoods in favour of the supposedly superior monastic life.

A true station might be that of farmer, shoe-maker, boy, girl, husband, wife, father, mother. If I am a housewife with four children that is my station. If I am a father and a shoemaker and a town councillor this too is my station. Each true station is endowed with honour and responsibility. A 'station' is not the same as what we mean by a 'job' or a 'career'. Some stations are clearly wrong and must be renounced, e.g. those of thief, prostitute or pimp. (Luther also felt bankers were dubious because they make money without working, as were monks because they live off the hard work of others!) But all the true stations are of equal dignity.

Luther's doctrine is open to the criticism that it legitimates fixed and oppressive social orders and working conditions: the peasant should jolly well do what he is told and stay in his field because that is where God has called him to be! We would certainly want to reject these suggestions today. The calling to a particular kind of work is fully compatible with a commitment to justice in the workplace. Furthermore, one's calling might develop and change. In our modern world it is quite common to receive callings to two or more different fields of work in the course of one's life.

Nonetheless, in its positive aspect, Luther's doctrine embodies a radical and, I think, profoundly Christ-like principle. Against our concerns with corporate (or indeed ecclesiastical) hierarchies Luther would have us insist that the status

---

1   For example, the sales of Sumitomo amount to about $150 bn p.a. compared to a GDP of $107 bn for Denmark, $52 bn for Greece and $32 bn for Ireland. (Figures from 'Times 1000' 1991/2 and OECD Survey 1991).

of the housewife, the preacher, the father, the soldier and the judge is equal. Each contributes in his or her own and distinctive way to the well being of the whole.

We can distinguish in Luther's doctrine four purposes for work.

- Firstly, God has ordained the stations as a means whereby he can perform his works of love on earth. In faithfully carrying out our offices we participate in God's love, in God's own care for human beings. Our vocation is thus directed first and foremost to our neighbour. Work is not primarily a means of being useful to God nor of developing ourselves, but it is rather the means by which we love other people.

- Secondly, God's own creative work is carried on through our work. For example, God gives the wool on the sheep, but it must be sheared, carded and spun by people in order to be the finished product that God intends.

- Thirdly, the stations compel our self-giving as an antidote to our natural selfishness. They perform the spiritual and character-building function of helping us learn obedience and self-denial.

- Fourthly, as a means of participation in the divine love and creativity, the stations are a sharing in joy.

Luther's doctrine of vocation challenges the modern idea that the main purpose of business life is to maximise profits. Of course profitability is necessary to be in business at all. But it is only a means to the greater end of creating valuable products which are expressions of love and service to our neighbours. From a Christian perspective, the moral worth of a business enterprise must always be the extent to which it raises the quality of human life and never the dividend it pays to shareholders. In our contemporary world, and going beyond Luther, a morally valuable business should also consider the *long term* effect of its activity on human life and the natural environment in which that life is lived.

Whilst insisting on the high purposes of work, Luther was, however, realistic about the difficulties and distress it may bring. Our calling places limits on our freedom of choice. The shoemaker is free to make shoes or not. However, he is not free to be a judge or to make jewellery. Luther himself had great doubts about his own vocation to be a preacher but felt compelled to continue with it. A calling demands perseverance.

Each workman face unique situations and moral dilemmas in his work. In their work men and women are, to some extent, on their own trying their best to live faithfully under the command of God. Living out one's calling is, moreover, a means of sharing in the suffering of Christ. Whether having one's sleep disrupted by babies, or coping with unruly subjects if one is a prince, or experiencing the contempt of the proud if one is a humble workman, all these are participations in the death of Christ. Says Luther, 'All Christians must suffer. You ask me where our suffering is to be found? I shall soon tell you. Run through all the stations of life...and you will find what you are looking for.'[1]

---

1   Luther *An die Pfarrherrn wider den Wucher zu predigen* p 404 (quoted in G Wingren, *The Christian's Calling* [Oliver and Boyd, Edinburgh 1958] p 29.

5
Ideas about Work in the Modern World

The Enlightenment marks a massive intellectual and philosophical shift in the way people view the natural world. No longer is it primarily the arena in which God acts and through which he reveals himself. Rather, man increasingly perceives himself alone to discover and define the rules of nature using empirical science and to exploit the natural realm to serve his own ends.

A notable figure in the Scottish Enlightenment was the deist Adam Smith, the founder of modern economics. He reversed the Reformation link between work and self-denial, in favour of a direct link between work and self-interest. 'It is not from the benevolence of the butcher, the brewer or the baker that we expect our dinner', he says, 'but from their regard to their own interest. We address ourselves not to their *humanity* but to their *self-love*. We never talk to them of our own needs but of their advantage.'[1] The important point here is that the theological justification for work has changed. The purpose of work is no longer that of lovingly producing goods for my neighbour. It is, rather, that of building up my own income. The value of work has become tied to the income it generates and severed from the worthiness of the product or service. As a consequence, work which brings in no income, such as voluntary work or the bringing up of children, is 'zero-rated'—it can scarcely be considered 'proper' work. Moreover, it now seems hard to see why anyone should work if they would be, as they say, 'better off' on the dole.[2]

Smith died just as the industrial revolution was getting underway. With the new economics working people become 'units of labour' to be bought at whatever price the market demanded. In the factories entrepreneurs brought together labour and capital to create wealth. The gross inhumanity of the working conditions in which this was done is well known. Workdays of 14 and 16 hours were normal. Little children as young as seven were carried to the factories by their parents as early as four o'clock in the morning and were often tied to the machines lest they fall asleep or run away.

The enlightenment and the industrial revolution form the immediate backdrop to two opposite and equally unhelpful views about work that emerge in the nineteenth and twentieth centuries.

---

1 Adam Smith *The Wealth of Nations* (1776) quoted in J Zylsrtra (ed) *Labour of Love* (Wedge, Ontario, 1980). Italics added.
2 None of this is, of course, to deny that sometimes, as a matter of practical economics, Smith's self-love and Luther's love of neighbour might coincide. My income may actually be maximised precisely by contributing most to the common good.

Work as 'Salvation'

Max Weber argued that Protestantism, with its emphasis on diligence, thrift, sobriety and prudence provided the climate in which hard work in pursuit of personal riches was legitimated.[1] This thesis is hotly contested.[2] Capitalism certainly cannot be traced back to Luther or Calvin, both of whom censured usury. It seems likely that other influences, not least the enlightenment attitude to the exploitation of nature, were also important in the formation of the modern capitalist work ethic. Nonetheless, for the American Puritans hard work was a divine mandate, while leisure was frowned upon. John Wesley extolled the spiritual benefits of hard work and a frugal lifestyle. Charles Spurgeon taught that labour was a shield against the temptations of the devil.

In a different vein, the nineteenth century romanticism of, for example, Thomas Carlyle, railed against the mechanisation and complexity of industrial working life and advocated a return to the idyllic work of mediaeval times. Here salvation might be found. 'There is a perennial nobleness, even sacredness in Work. It has been written, "an endless significance lies in Work"; a man perfects himself by working. Consider how, even in the meanest sorts of Labour, the whole soul of a man is composed into a kind of real harmony, the instance he sets himself to work!...The blessed glow of Labour in him, is it not as purifying fire, wherein all poison is burnt up, and of sour smoke itself there is made bright blessed flame!'[3]

Carlyle's capitalisation of 'Labour' and 'Work' looks ominous when we are aware of what later totalitarian political movements were to make of the purifying character of work. Chinese and Russian communist governments sent their dissidents to labour camps. Inmates were expected to be cleansed and made fit to take their place in socialist society. A similar attitude prevailed in Nazism: the slogan on the gates of Auschwitz read *Arbeit Macht Frei* (labour makes free). It is apparently through work that one is liberated and saved.

In our own society we might consider the phenomenon of workaholism. At an individual level, a person may run away from family problems, from loneliness or from facing up to themselves by burying themselves in their work. Workaholics can be found equally amongst the ranks of company executives, the clergy and the self-employed. At an institutional level, some enterprises (I am thinking particularly of some of the professional services firms such as city accountants and commercial lawyers) may sustain a corporate ethos or culture that carries a *de facto* salvific role. The employee is promised a very high salary and abundant job satisfaction provided only that the employee gives the firm total commitment in such matters as working hours and mobility.

---

1   *The Protestant Work Ethic and the Spirit of Capitalism* ET 1930.
2   For example see David Attwood's discussion in the Grove Ethics Series.
3   Thomas Carlyle, *Past and Present* (1843) Bk III Ch XI quoted on p 241 of A Clayre (ed) *Nature and Industrialisation* (OUP, 1977).

I take it that all attempts to over-exalt the role of work are breaches of the first commandment: 'I am the Lord your God who brought you out of the land of Egypt, out of the house of bondage. You shall have no other gods before me' (Ex 20:2).

Work as Dis-Benefit

The nineteenth century philosopher Jeremy Bentham held that pleasure and pain are the measure of all things, including standards of right and wrong. According to his principle of utility work is a painful disbenefit ('evil') whilst its end, the possession of goods, or its cessation, rest, is a pleasurable benefit ('good').

'*Aversion*—not *desire*—is the emotion—the only emotion—which *labour*, taken by itself, is qualified to produce: of any such emotion as *love* or *desire, ease*, which is the *negative* or *absence* of labour—*ease*, not *labour*—is the object. In so far as *labour* is taken in its proper sense, love of labour is a contradiction in terms.'[1]

This view, whilst deeply opposed to the Christian understanding of work, has proved at least as popular as its opposite 'Work as Salvation'. If the latter is summed up in the slogan 'You live to work', the former is 'You work to live'.

Much of 1960s and 1970s industrial relations was characterised by the notion that work is a disbenefit, simply an unpleasant means to the pleasurable ends of personal income or corporate profit. The labourer's work becomes the pivot on which the opposing goods of private and corporate gain are balanced and negotiated. We get the language of productivity agreements, of demarcation disputes and of bonuses.

The traditional car factory production line seems to me to be the embodiment of work reduced to the level of dis-benefit. Huw Beynon offered a particularly sharp description of what it is like to work in a car factory in his contribution to industrial sociology 'Working for Ford':

> 'If you stand on the cat-walk at the end of the plant you can look down over the whole assembly floor. Few people do, for to stand there and look at the endless, perpetual tedium of it all is to be threatened by the overwhelming insanity of it all. The sheer audacious madness of a system based on men like these wishing their lives away...It's the most boring job in the world. It's the same thing over and over again. There's no change in it. It wears you out. It makes you awful tired. It slows your thinking right down. There's no need to think. It's just a formality. You just carry on. You just endure it for the money. That's what we're paid for—to endure the boredom of it...It's different for them in the office. They are part of Ford. We are not. We are numbers.'[2]

To make the point once more, Ernst Schumacher quotes an article from the Times, 'Dante, when composing his visions of hell might well have included the mindless, repetitive boredom of working in a factory assembly line. It destroys

1 Jeremy Bentham *A Table from the Springs of Action* (1817) p 20. Quoted in Clayre p 200.
2 H Beynon *Working for Ford* (Penguin, 1984) p 119,129,132.

initiative and rots brains, yet millions of British workers are committed to it for most of their lives.'[1] The astonishing thing is, says Schumacher, that no-one wrote into the Times to oppose the article. These conditions of working life were apparently accepted as 'normal'.

Recalling the four purposes of work we found in Luther (Section 3) we realise that work is no longer experienced as service to neighbour. It is no longer perceived as a sharing in God's creativity. It is found to be destructive rather than constructive of character. And it is supremely lacking in joy. In a *consumer* society work is a dis-benefit which must be endured in order that we may acquire things. In this context, *efficiency* becomes a pressing concern. How do we make the most things for the least labour? How do we maximise our pleasure for the least pain? But in the rush to consume, little attention is paid to what is being done to the minds and souls of the producers.

---

1   E Schumacher *Good Work* (Jonathan Cape, 1979) p 1.

6
Towards a Contemporary Theology of Work

Inadequate Theological Responses of Withdrawal

Modern society consists of an enormous diversity of workplaces. Some corporations have huge economic power. Modern-day work may appear for some
to be so enriching and absorbing as to be a kind of salvation, and for others to be
so tedious and routine as to be dehumanising. Faced with such complexity the
church may take at least two defensive steps.

Firstly it may define itself as identical with the Kingdom of God in opposition to 'the world'. Inside it is all light; outside is only darkness. The workplace
is now primarily of value either as a locus of evangelism or as a potential source
of funds to build up the church. Christians, if they are truly faithful, will seek to
find a vocation in some kind of position of service within the church. Their
secular work is carried on so as to support themselves, their families and their
church. A positive contribution to modern working life could, perhaps, be made
through setting up or joining a 'Christian' business which might act as a particular kind of witness. But such teaching as the church offers in respect of work
will mainly be exhortations to workers to find opportunities at work to witness
to their faith. Work will be regarded as unhelpful to the extent that it draws
Christians away from church-based activities.

I suggest that this is an inadequate response. It fails completely to take seriously the rich Christian (and especially Protestant) doctrine of vocation derived
from scripture and articulated by Luther. It makes too simple a split between
the action of God in the church and in the world. Finally it does not accord with
the empirical reality of either the workplace or the church.

A second defensive measure is to hark back to a less developed form of life.
This could be a variant on the romantic yearning for mediaeval forms of social
organisation and patterns of work that we saw advocated in the last century by
Carlyle. The presence of God is now thought to be found wherever there is
simplicity. The church withdraws support for the modern world and encourages
its members to opt-out.

I have more sympathy with this move, since it seems to me there is a clear
place for alternative patterns of life which protest against the exploitation of
natural and human resources that highly developed societies can entail. However, it can never be more than a *partial* response. There is much about modern
life, including working life, that Christians will wish to affirm. For example,
working conditions are undeniably better for most people now than they were
in previous centuries. Many of the material blessings of modern life (such as
electricity or advanced health care) require large-scale and complex methods of
production and distribution. The presence of God must be discerned and cel-
ebrated precisely in the complexity and diversity of modern working life.

A Better Response: Starting With Trinity and Creation

A contemporary doctrine of work will have to begin with the great doctrines of Trinity and creation. Unless we are able to see the creative purposes of God at work in the whole of his creation we are unlikely to make much progress in the particular sphere of work. Until very recently both Catholic and Protestant theology has neglected the doctrine of Creation, or at any rate treated as only a preface to doctrines of covenant and redemption.[1] Within Protestant theology this deficiency has been addressed particularly forcefully by Jürgen Moltmann.

Moltmann wishes to move us away from conceiving of the monotheistic God who is transcendent from his creation towards the Trinitarian God who is deeply and intricately related to the world. The world is created by God the Father, formed through God the Son and exists in God the Holy Spirit. In his recent book *God in Creation*, and relying partly on the Jewish notion of *Shekinah*, Moltmann directs us particularly to the neglected immanence of God the Creator Spirit and the great variety of relationships between God and his creation that this entails.

If we make the Sovereignty of God our supreme theological principle (as Karl Barth did) then Moltmann argues that we inevitably produce a series of antitheses, for example between God and the world, heaven and earth, soul and body. In the terms of this paper the antitheses are continued in an opposition between church and workplace. These antitheses are only overcome through a proper doctrine of God as Trinity.

For Moltmann, if God is understood to be a community of persons existing in mutual relationships of love, it now makes sense to talk not simply of human individuals being made in the image of God, but of human communities bearing a social likeness to God.[2] These communities range from the very simple primal community of Adam and Eve to the highly interrelated and sophisticated workplace communities of the modern world.

Now the classical doctrine of the Trinity was formulated at a time when it seemed obvious from Greek philosophy that God was a motionless being. But the notion that the divine Trinity is *dynamic* seems to fit better both with the Biblical picture of God and with what we know about the nature of ultimate reality from modern science. In modern theology it is Prof. Daniel Hardy who has reflected the most deeply on the Trinity's dynamic character.[3] God is continually realising new possibilities of existence within his own Trinitarian relationships and in his relationships with world. It is the Spirit who provides the creative energy for these new possibilities. Hardy argues that, through his ongoing interaction with society, the Spirit provides the 'kinetic energy' through

---

1   So Karl Rahner (*Sacramentum Mundi* Vol. II pp 23-37) and Karl Barth's *Church Dogmatics*
2   J Moltmann *God in Creation* (SCM 1985) p 234ff.
3   D W Hardy was formerly professor of systematic theology at the university of Durham and is a past president of the British Society for the Study of Theology. He is currently Director of the Centre for Theological Inquiry at Princeton, USA. My comments are based on his lectures at Durham. His ideas are set out more fully in D W Hardy and D F Ford *Jubilate: Theology in Praise* (London, 1984, but, unfortunately, currently out of print).

which society is built up. The Spirit is thus understood to be deeply involved in the change, diversity and complexity of modern life, and not least modern working life.

The Spirit, Social Codes and Corporate Culture

Just as energy builds up physical and chemical structures in the natural world, so Hardy suggests that the interaction between God the Spirit and human society takes place especially through the production of a social structure or 'social code'. Social codes would include both formal rules such as laws and standards of ethics, and informal conventions, organisational structures and means of decision making. Through human work in accordance with such codes the creative purposes of the Trinity may be achieved. Good codes enable the possibilities of society to be realised, they help people to feel at home and contented in their society and they are just.

Social groups may, however, attempt to structure themselves without reference to the energy of the Spirit. This is made visible in attempts at encapsulation of one kind or another. A group may encapsulate itself from nature, pretending that its activities can be carried on regardless of their effect on the natural world. It may shut itself off from its links with the past or the implications of its conduct for the future. It may deliberately marginalise or exclude certain individuals. On the other hand it may focus so much on the needs of individuals that it is unconcerned for the wider society. In each case the 'social codes' fail to maximise the possibilities of the created order, breed discontent and are found to be unjust.

In the work place the idea of 'social codes' translates into what we know as corporate culture. These cultures may develop unconsciously and be implicit and unstated. In my previous firm the culture was carefully developed and sustained and highly explicit. Parts of a culture will be formal and written down, for example personnel policies and procedures, codes of practice and organisation charts. Other parts are less formal and more a matter of 'how we do things here'. Some components of the culture will be ethically neutral but are still important in setting the tone of the organisation. For example my former company had a (as far as I am aware unwritten) rule that all staff of whatever grade addressed each other by first names. Other components will have a clear ethical significance, for example, the implicit or explicit rule that 'we always do a high quality job'.

Corporate cultures are communicated through written directives and informal contact and example. Japanese and American companies have mottoes, mission statements and even songs to maintain the culture. Cultures are transmitted especially through training. At least part of the attachment the Church of England feels towards its theological colleges is surely that they are a reliable means of enculturating ordinands. These colleges have their parallels in the induction courses of commercial enterprises and the basic training of the armed services. Someone who has not been through this process of induction may always be suspected of not understanding quite fully enough what 'we' are about.

Corporate culture is of enormous importance. It could be said to lie at the heart of the debates about nationalised industries. It profoundly affects what a work organisation feels like to work in, how contented employees feel in their work, and what a company's stance on moral issues is likely to be. It is through the operation of culture that we can understand Schumacher's comment that, 'A person's work is undoubtedly one of the most formative influences on their character and personality'.[1] The central role of corporate culture may well lead us to identify it as the *spirit* of the corporation,[2] a spirit which may be more or less aligned with the Creator Spirit. A rotten or ossified corporate culture pervades a whole organisation like a bad smell. In this extreme case we may wish to talk of a culture having an evil spirit.

Discerning the spirit or culture of the corporation is primarily a matter of testing its fruit. In brief, good cultures *maximise the possibilities inherent in people and natural resources with regard to the widest ecological, societal and temporal horizons.* As such they may be said to be attuned to the energising power of the Spirit—whether or not this power is explicitly recognised. Good cultures produce 'wealth' (a word linked etymologically to wellness or health) in the widest sense: they develop the potential of the natural world, they supply high quality goods at a reasonable price to those who need them, and they embody an attitude of care to employees. Given the great diversity of work to be done, and the range of gifts and personalities different people bring to their work it is difficult to define good culture in more than general terms. We cannot, for example, say that small firms are better than large ones: both kinds have equal potential for good or oppressive cultures. We might, though, say that some kinds of activity (such as specialist software development) are *appropriate* to small firms in a way that other activities (such as oil exploration) are appropriate to large firms. Neither could we say that a highly enterprising culture is always better than a more stable, bureaucratic one: some people are liberated by the former, others may be deeply threatened by it.

Much current discontent in the workplace arises from the political insistence that one form of corporate culture, that of the entrepreneurial company, ought to be applied to all work organisations including those, such as the police, the health service and education services, which have traditionally embodied the very different culture of public service. Against this I would argue that, just as the Spirit gives a variety of gifts, so he animates a diversity of work cultures. It seems to me obvious that the kind of culture suitable, for example, for the trading of financial futures, will be quite different from one suitable for the education of young children. Calculated risk-taking is central to the former but mostly quite out of place in the latter. The insistence that one form of culture is superior

---

1   Schumacher, p 3.
2   Following my colleague Justin Welby's suggestion in his Grove Ethics booklet *Can Companies Sin?*

to all the others serves to devalue and demotivate those whose work embodies a different ethos. I would want to insist, in particular, that fundamentally different attitudes are required when the 'product' is a human being rather than a material artefact. Why did I feel uncomfortable when the superintendent of the local crematorium told me he was running a process industry whose performance could be measured by its throughput? It was because I feared he had temporarily forgotten that people, even dead people, have an inherent dignity which requires them to be treated and spoken about in an essentially different way from 'things'.

A related issue concerns the current pace of cultural change in the workplace. The Spirit is the dynamic Creator Spirit who refuses to allow us to become fixed in our codes and structures. Yet he is also the Spirit of gentleness. Attempts to impose large-scale changes to corporate cultures in a short space of time typically generate huge levels of stress for employees. Work loads increase owing to the need to keep existing procedures going at the same time as learning new procedures and practices. Ways that had become familiar through habitual practice have to be relearned. The management and implementation of change is the task of those at the top of the corporate hierarchy. It is a demanding task, requiring imagination, careful planning and effective communication if people are not to be hurt, sometimes badly, in the process.

To summarise: a good culture would seem to offer workers a high potential for realising the benefits of work that we saw identified in Luther, namely, sharing in God's creativity, active love of neighbour, growth in character and sharing in divine joy. It would not, however, eliminate the unpleasant aspects of work that Luther also identified. Firstly, in this world there is always likely to be some degree of mismatch between the personal preferences and abilities of an individual and the range of occupations and cultural environments open to them. Secondly suffering (be it physical or mental) will always be a part of work. Thirdly, work will always entail a certain ethical loneliness as workers necessarily face a stream of unique moral choices and dilemmas in the course of their work. Precisely because work is *my* vocation, I bear the responsibility for working out for myself what a Christlike action would be in the particular circumstances I face, and I cannot shuffle this responsibility onto my colleagues, the Church or the wider society.